How to Build a Better Mousetrap

Recollections and Reflections of a Family Caregiver

Poems by
Abbie Johnson Taylor

iUniverse, Inc.
Bloomington

How to Build a Better Mousetrap
Recollections and Reflections of a Family Caregiver

iUniverse books may be ordered through booksellers or by contacting:

iUniverse
1663 Liberty Drive
Bloomington, IN 47403
www.iuniverse.com
1-800-Authors (1-800-288-4677)

ISBN: 978-1-4620-6794-7 (sc)
ISBN: 978-1-4620-6795-4 (e)
Printed in the United States of America

iUniverse rev. date: 11/23/2011

Acknowledgments

I would like to acknowledge the publications in which the following poems appeared,: "The Bedroom," and "Dear Bill" in *Peninsula Poets*: "Timber!" "Awaiting the Return of the Better Half," and "While Walking Home" in *Wordgathering*: "Socks" in *Southwest Women's Poetry Exchange*: "Reta's Song" in *Serendipity Poets Journal*, "Coming Home" in *Voicings from the High Country*, and "Ducks on the Sidewalk" and "A Story After Noon" in *Distant Horizons*.

I would like to thank the following employees of the Sheridan Senior Citizens Center for their help with this project: Bunni Ruby, our caseworker with the in-home services program, for inspiring this book's title and Nancy McKenzie, volunteer coordinator, for the photo of me and my husband on the cover. I would also like to thank the following: participants in my monthly poetry group for their inspiration and feedback, and my totally blind husband Bill, partially paralyzed as a result of two strokes, for being an unwilling subject of my poetry.

Last but not least, I would like to acknowledge residents at Sheridan Manor, a nursing home where I worked as an activities assistant for fifteen years before writing full time. Those who lived there during my employment are now gone, but they inspired the poems in the last part of this book.

Contents

Part 1
On Being a Family Caregiver

The Day My Husband Had a Stroke

It's about a quarter to twelve on Saturday, January 28th, 2006.
I'm walking downtown where I'll meet a friend for lunch.
Afterward, I'll come home, finish laundry,
read a book, anticipate the spaghetti dinner he'll fix later.
At four o'clock, I'll listen to "A Prairie Home Companion."
At six, I'll meet others in my singing group at the Eagles Club
where we'll perform for a wine tasting.
At seven, I'll come home, expect to find supper on the table—
instead, he'll be lying on the floor.
Our lives won't be the same.

Hemorrhage

Barely coherent, drenched in sweat, he lay on the floor. "What happened?" I asked. His response was unintelligible.

"I don't need to go to the hospital," he told the paramedics. "but if my wife wants me to go, I guess I will."

"The stroke was caused by bleeding on the right side of his brain," said the doctor. "He may need surgery."

"In this case, surgery won't help," another doctor told us. "We'll just have to wait and see."

"He's not strong enough to participate in our rehabilitation program," said the social worker. "He'll have to go to a nursing home."

"I don't know how much you'll recover or how long it will take," a third doctor said. "Continue the therapy, and watch your blood pressure."

"We'll work on strengthening your legs and try to get you up and moving," the therapist promised him.

"They've given up on me. I don't think I'll ever walk again."

A Secret Sadness

I fight to keep from crying.
"Push it back, way back," I tell myself.
Melissa's eight-year-old cries of delight
mingle with the chatter of her playmates,
the smell of tacos.

Bill suffered a stroke that paralyzed his left side.
Will he ever walk again?

I paste a smile on my face, admire Melissa's presents.
How can I be happy?

Dependent

I know what to do—
I don't know what to do.
The wheelchair, vertical bars, gait belt
offer assistance but can't bring him back.
He's not the man I married—
he's still the man I love.

Stroke

I owe you a million kisses.
I owe you a million hugs—
and now that you are my Mrs.,
I should keep you safe from thugs.
But I have been dealt a hard blow
which leaves me unable to do
the things I delighted in so,
and that includes loving you.
If I could hold you once more,
I'd cherish the love you provide.
If fate would open the door
and allow me to walk inside,
    I'd give you a million kisses
    now that you are my Mrs.

The Bedroom

At three in the morning,
I'm mildly aroused
by the gentle touch of his hand.
He only has one good arm and leg
but still knows how to please me.
As he strokes me,
and I breathe the scent of his sweat,
I purr with anticipation.
The mood is shattered
when he whispers, "I need to pee."

Bliss

"Just give me one more hour of sleep,"
I silently pray
to my husband, unable to care for himself,
my body, the world in general.

It's eight in the morning.
I lie with my eyes closed,
enjoy the Sunday morning peace.
It doesn't last.

Timber!

We hear the workmen next door,
as we get ready for our day.
Lying down, we put on his pants,
one leg, then the other,
roll, pull, roll, pull
till they're up as far as they'll go.

Sitting on the side of the bed,
we remove his sweaty t-shirt.
His arm encircles my waist.
We tug, laugh,
swear till it's over his head.
One arm, then the other,
it's off.

On goes the sweatshirt,
one sleeve, then the other,
over his head it goes.

All the while,
chain saws whine.
Branches and limbs fall,
bring change, welcome or not.

Solitude

His side of the bed is empty.
An open space replaces his wheelchair.
His recliner stands vacant.

He's a victim of fate
in the form of another cerebral bleed,
not as bad as before.

I'm alone.
The house is quiet, empty, still
with one less meal to fix,
one less person here.

Dear Bill

I believe that one day, you'll walk through the door,
take me in your arms. We'll embrace.
What happened a year ago
was a major obstacle flung in our path to wedded bliss.
What happened yesterday was only a small setback.
I knew that, as I sat by your hospital bed.
We laughed, talked.
You dozed from time to time.
I tried to kiss you.
My lips couldn't reach yours through the side rail.
You reached out, stroked my hair, told me not to worry.

So as I did last year,
I'll lead my lone existence,
get up in the morning,
make breakfast for one instead of two,
go about my day,
visit you when I can,
go to sleep in my lonely bed,
know that you'll soon be next to me.
I believe that some day, you'll walk through the door,
take me in your arms, hold me.
I'll live for that day.

From a Husband's Perspective

She works hard
to care for me, the house.
She cooks, cleans, does laundry,
fetches, carries,
does everything I'm unable to do.
She writes short stories, novels, essays.
She'll be a best selling author one day.
I couldn't do without her.

Before I Leave

He's cranky, doesn't want lunch,
then asks for vegetable beef soup.
It has no beef.
I give him my sandwich.
It falls apart.
He gives up on lunch.

As I'm leaving, he's reclining,
a chocolate in his mouth, a bag of almonds on his lap.
His good arm encircles my neck.
We laugh, as we kiss goodbye.

Recumbent

With his good hand, he presses a button.
The chair reclines.
Familiar objects are within reach,
telephone, radio, drink,
cassette player, bag of nuts, TV remote control.
As I cover him with poncho and blanket,
his sightless eyes gaze at me with love.
He smiles, content.

While Walking Home

As my long white cane rolls from side to side in front of me,
I feel the sun, the gentle breezes that caress my face.
I should hurry, but what's the rush?
The sun shines in a cloudless sky.
The air is warm, permeated with the scent of roses.
He's been home alone for three hours.
Fifteen minutes more won't matter, will it?

When I get home, I'll take him outside in his wheelchair
so he can enjoy the late afternoon sun,
flop into my armchair in the living room with my feet up,
kick off my shoes, drink Dr. Pepper
while downloading e-mail onto my Victor Stream.
Its synthetic voice will read to me,
as I fold and put away laundry, prepare dinner.
We'll eat together, content,
as another day draws to a close.

Awaiting The Return
of the Better Half

The phone rings.
With his right hand, the only one that works,
he presses the talk button on the cordless unit,
slowly lifts it to his ear, says, "Hello."
"Hi, honey," I say.
I'll be home in fifteen minutes."
He places the phone next to him on the bed,
presses the talk button a second time to disconnect the call.

A container filled with urine balances between his legs.
He listens to his recorded book, anticipates my return.

Finally, the kitchen door opens, closes.
He hears me moving around,
wonders why I don't come to him.
He picks up the phone, dials my cell.
"I'm here," I tell him.
"I'm putting my things away.
I'll be right there."

When I enter the room with a cheerful greeting, we embrace.
He tries unsuccessfully to kiss me while laughing.
Then, offering the urinal, he says,
"I've got something for you."

Before and After

In the beginning, you knew all about me,
which buttons to push,
how to hook me up,
install programs, fix problems.

Now, you hesitate,
push the wrong buttons.
When I don't give you the desired response,
you beat my keyboard, proclaim I don't work.

I needed new parts because I was slow to start.
You had them installed.
Still, you become frustrated
when I don't perform the desired function.

I wish I could read your thoughts,
still want to please you.

Urgent!

I know you're busy, but this is important.
I realize you don't want to be interrupted,
but I have something to tell you that can't wait.
Your voice on your cell phone's answering system is reassuring.
Hurry home.
I miss you, your touch, your kiss.
You are my angel, my dove, my everything.
There's no one else I cherish more than you.

The Sun Shines When You Laugh

Storm clouds part, drift away,
reveal a blue sky.
The wind diminishes to a gentle breeze,
rustles tree branches, wind chimes.
Birds sing happy tunes.
Crows caw in the distance.
Squirrels and insects skitter from place to place,
delighted to be alive.
All is peaceful.

Reassurance

Loving, caring, sensitive,
with gentle kisses and caresses,
he knows how to make me feel good
although he can only use one arm and leg.

When I press my face to his cheek,
drink in his sweet aroma,
my worries and doubts melt away.

When You're Not Here

I listen to your music,
hear longing in the words,
    sit in your chair
surrounded by the warmth,
    eat your favorite food,
know your pleasure in the taste,
    drink your beverage of choice.
My thirst isn't quenched.
I imagine your body next to mine.
You're not here.

Awakening

I open my eyes,
gaze upon his sweet sleeping face,
long to hold, kiss him,
caress his hair, his cheek.
He stirs, says, "Good morning."
We embrace, happy.

Time Travel

I scrub the grill—my husband sits at the table,
eats a dinner roll, drinks a Pepsi.
I do all the housework—
he supervises, relaxes, sleeps.
If he could share household duties, he would—
but he only has the use of one arm and leg.

In the nineteenth century, women did household chores—
men remained sedentary when not working.
I'm a twenty-first century woman in a nineteenth century world—
I wouldn't have it any other way.

Spring's Hopelessness

Spring comes wet with little sun. Hope is dashed by the wind that buffets the house, rattles wind chimes, rain that drums on the roof. Without enough warmth, grass, flowers, trees, shrubs won't grow.

He loves the sun, can't get enough. It's one of his few pleasures since he can no longer walk or use his left arm or care for himself. After a brutal winter with endless snow, frigid temperatures, he longs to enjoy the sun's healing warmth.

wishes for the sun
fall on the deaf ears of God
wait for warmth to come

Things I'll Never Tell You

I'll never tell you you're stupid
when you forget something or don't understand.
I'll never tell you you're lazy
when you sit at the kitchen table in your wheelchair
while I fix dinner, clean up.
I'll never tell you you're a baby
when I must do most things for you.
I'll never tell you I don't understand
why you can't walk and do more for yourself
when I know the reason.
I'll never tell you I hate you
or that I was a fool to marry you.
You can't help being the way you are.
I'll always love you—although the vow was never spoken,
I'll be with you for better or worse.

Ending The Day

As evening shadows lengthen,
I remove his shoes and socks, pull off his shirt.
As I drag his pants over his hips,
buttocks, thighs, he laughs.
He says it's funny.
I think he's embarrassed.
As I tuck him in,
we kiss and say I love you.
I climb in beside him,
hold him, bury my face in his hair,
drink in the scent of his shampoo.
I'm soon lulled to sleep by his gentle, even breathing.

I Dream of Being Rich

If I were a millionaire,
I'd buy us a big house in California with a swimming pool,
make it accessible to your wheelchair,
hire a therapist to work with you,
attendants to see to your personal care,
a staff of servants to cook and clean.
I could focus on writing.
We could enjoy each other's company,
free from worries about social security and insurance.

Turning Point

At times, I say, "I married the most wonderful man.
How did that happen?"
There's something about the way he laughs
when he's happy, sad, embarrassed,
the way his good arm encircles me,
as I walk by his wheelchair,
and his hand strokes my hair.
Even his bodily functions are cute.

At times, I ask myself, "Why am I doing this?
Why don't I put him in a home and go about my business?"
In answer, he tells me he loves me,
kisses me, laughs,
fails to kiss me again through his laughter.
Our lives are still worthwhile.

Part 2

Recollections

On Being Three

I barely remember that year.
Mother said my first word was ashtray.
That's funny—I've never smoked.
My earliest memory is of Dad cursing a blue streak.
Hmm—maybe he swore because I broke his ashtray.

On Top of The House

The cooler stands silent, inert,
dares Dad to fix it.
At the age of eight, I perch on one of the roof's slopes,
gaze in wonder at the world below.
Mother calls from far away, yet close.
Where is she?

Dad hunches over the cooler.
"Turn it on," he calls.
After a pause, it springs to life,
distributing cool air throughout the house's interior.
It's time to leave the top of the world.

Highland Adventure

Mother packs sandwiches, chips, fruit, pop,
loads everything into the trunk of our Mercedes Benz.
Dad turns off the air conditioner.
We open the windows, breathe the fresh mountain air.
We picnic near a creek.
My younger brother, father, and I dabble in the water.
When it's too deep, I'm afraid.
Dad holds me, tells me to kick.
Later, we pile into the car, tired but happy.
My brother and I are asleep before we reach home.

A Memorable Stop in Colorado

In the summer of 1971 at the age of ten,
I traveled with Dad from our home in Tucson, Arizona,
to Sheridan, Wyoming, to visit Grandma.
While bar hopping in Durango,
I had Coke—Dad drank something stronger.
One establishment served hot dogs.
I liked them plain with not even a bun.
I must have had at least three.
Intoxicated, we made our way to the car.
I slept on the back seat
while Dad slept on the ground nearby.
Who knows where we were when we woke up?

Socks

At the age of eleven,
I sit on the floor in front of the wastebasket in my room,
pull loose threads from my socks, one by one.

"What are these sock strings doing on the floor?" Mother asks.
    "The cat did it," I say.

Despite continual chastisement and threats of spanking,
my favorite pastime is removing threads from my socks, one by one.

In the Garden

There are no trees, just an expanse of dirt.
While Mother and Dad work, I sit on the steps,
study seed packets of peas, corn, tomatoes,
read the labels, gaze at the pictures.
I'm only twelve.

In the distance, sirens wail.
"It sounds like fire engines," says Dad.

In the house, the phone rings.
I hurry to answer it.
A male voice asks for my mother.
I rush outside, call her to the phone,

"Oh my god! We'll be right there."
    "Ed, we need to pick up Andy at the police station.
He was playing with matches near that shack
at the bottom of the hill when it caught fire."
The garden is abandoned.

Junior High

School
bells ring.
Students yell.
Locker doors slam.
Buses thrum nearby,
bring children from afar
to classrooms, waiting teachers
in a school atmosphere controlled
by a fat and sassy principal.

The Music Room

After one crew removed the old room,
another poured cement, created a floor, walls, windows, roof.
Carpeting was laid.
The piano, drum set, and stereo were installed.
A love seat and Franklin stove were purchased.
For years, we played together in that room,
me on piano, my brother on drums.
We eventually went our separate ways—
the house was sold—
we still remember.

Sock Ceremony

Balancing on the edge of the washing machine,
Wanda reaches into its depth,
retrieves a dirty sock,
jumps down, places it on the floor.
"Meow, meow," she says,
as she circles it once or twice.
She walks away,
leaves it for someone else to find.

Leaf Disposal

We gathered them into bags, placed them curbside. Mother said, "We used to burn the leaves. It was the smell of fall. Let's burn a few now."

It had been a dry year. Forest fires raged around us. I couldn't remember the last time it rained. "I don't think this is a good idea," I said.

"Stop being such a chicken. Help me gather leaves into a pile." With a sick feeling in my stomach, I did as I was told.

She struck a match—nothing happened. The wind came up. Leaves drifted away, as if they knew of their fate. She tried again with no results. After several more tries, she gave up, to my relief. We got rid of the leaves in the usual way.

Winter

On a cold, cloudy day, we strap on our skis, boots, head up the trail. I inch along, sure I'll fall at any minute, as my skis slide through the packed snow. "Left foot right pole right foot left pole. See if you can go faster," Dad says. I prefer to keep my slow, plodding pace.

At the top of the hill, we retrace our steps. My feet slide out from under me. I land flat on my back. "Smile," says my brother, as he holds the camera.

"Stick that camera where the sun won't shine," I want to tell him.

"You're not falling right. You could get hurt," he says. I remove the skis, walk the rest of the day.

Coming Home

The car turns onto the dirt road and stops.
The rear left passenger door opens.
Out jumps an Irish setter.
The door slams shut.
The car moves down the road at a moderate pace.

The dog runs alongside the car,
her red, floppy ears and mane blowing in the breeze,
the multi-colored kerchief around her neck visible in the sunlight.
She hesitates, sniffs something along the side of the road.
The car stops—Dad calls, "Come on Maud."
Maud turns toward the car—we're off.

About a mile down the road,
    the car turns into the driveway of a log cabin—
Mother hurries out to meet us.
Maud rushes up to her, tail wagging in frantic anticipation.
She strokes the dog's shaggy neck—
Maud gives her a sloppy kiss.
She runs in joyous circles around the car,
as we alight and items are removed from the trunk.
It's so good to be home!

Remembering an Irish Setter Long Gone

Maud hurries from the house to greet me.
Her tail thumps against my leg in welcome.
I bend, scratch behind her floppy ears,
bury my face in her red fur,
drink in her dog scent.
After an especially hard day at work
when I break down, weep,
she washes away my tears.

Departure

We kiss in the rain
while the bus thrums nearby,
waiting to take you away.
"What's this hood?" you ask, as our lips meet.
I try to remove it.
"Keep it on," you say, as I yield.
I hold you, will the bus to leave without you.
All too soon, you're gone.

Speeding

I'm sitting in a car going over ninety miles an hour. "If I stay behind this car, I won't speed," Dad says. "It's going under the speed limit." But the car in front of us turns off at the next exit. The speedometer climbs.

"God damn it," he says, as he slows down. "I just want to get home."

"So do I, but I want to make it in one piece."

"Fuck you! I'm tired."

"And you don't think I am?" I want to tell him. "You don't think it's exhausting, speeding down the highway with you, watching you fiddle with the tape deck and consult a road map when both hands should be on the wheel, your eyes glued to the road?" Hallelujah! We're home at last!

Belch!

The room is silent
but for the scratch of pencil against paper,
murmur of voices,
flip, rip of pages.
Unexpected, it cuts through the silence,
raucous, obnoxious,
breaks my concentration.
I fight to diffuse a bomb of mirth
that threatens to explode.
The effort brings tears to my eyes.
After a moment, I continue writing,
but my heart's not in it anymore.

The Blue Doorknob

"Ting a-ling, ting a-ling," goes the cell phone.
With an apology, someone hurries from the room.
Better him than me, I think,
as I try to concentrate.
I forgot to turn mine off.
"What comes to mind when you think of a blue doorknob," asks the
poet.
The one in my pocket threatens to expose me
or inspire someone to write a poem.

Part 3
Reflections

A Spring Constitutional

In the early morning, a cold wind blows.
The weak sunlight from a hazy sky offers little warmth.
Despite the chill in the air, I'm glad to be out walking.
I smell fresh new-mown grass and hear bird songs.
In the park, a workman mows the lawn.
There's no one else in sight.

I walk by the creek, hear its gentle babble,
the neighing of horses from a nearby veterinary clinic,
smell the manure.
My white cane rolls from side to side in front of me.

In the late afternoon, I traverse the same path,
relieved to be out in the fresh air.
I hear the cries of children from the nearby playground.
My stomach tells me I'm hungry.
I quicken my pace, eager to reach home.

On A Summer Evening

Cool
darkness
surrounds me.
Crickets chirp their
evening serenade.
I lie awake, listen
to the night outside the panes.
I finally close my eyes and drift,
lulled by the crickets' songs, the breezes.

I Admire My Handiwork

The poem contains nine lines,
each with one more syllable than the last.
It looks like a Christmas tree.
I'm transported back to my fifth grade classroom
in a school for children with visual impairments.

I'm pasting pop bottle tops to a piece of red felt
in nine rows, each containing more lids than the last.
But the rows are jagged.
"It's supposed to look like a Christmas tree," says Mrs. Jones.
"Don't you know what a Christmas tree looks like?"

Almost fifty years later,
I stare in amazement at my computer screen
where I've managed to form a perfect Christmas tree out of words.

Breakfast

We eat pancakes,
not square, not triangular,
not bathed in peanut butter or onions,
round buttermilk pancakes
covered with maple syrup,
prepared by me with love.

Inside A Sandwich

Lunchmeat, cheese, lettuce, onions,
tomatoes, mayonnaise abound.
When that's all gone, there's only bread.
In the absence of dough, there's nothing but hunger.

An Italian Meal without Wine

I love to eat seafood fettuccini Alfredo,
taste the shrimp, crab, scallops
in a rich, creamy sauce
on a bed of fettuccini noodles,
slurp the noodles into my mouth,
savor the flavor,
garnish it with garlic bread,
chase it down with water.

Ode to Dr. Pepper

I like to swallow its cold carbonation,
feel it come back into my mouth in the form of a belch.
Oh, that feels so good!

I drink it in mid afternoon.
It helps me get through the day.
I sometimes consume it in the evening
when I'm sleepy, and it's too early for bed.

In the good old days,
I drank a lot of it,
just what the doctor ordered.
Now, the doctor says it has too much sugar
so I limit my consumption to one or two cans a day.
What would I do without it?

Dear Julie

I wonder what you think, as you read me my e-mail,
the Web pages I browse, other documents.
Is there something you'd rather not read to me,
something I don't want read that interests you?
When you repeat what I type,
how do the words strike you?
When I shut down, are you relieved or disappointed?
When I boot up, do you sigh with resignation
or jump at the chance of helping me again?
Now, I'll ask you to read this back to me.
Knowing it's about you, will you blush?

Ducks on the Sidewalk

Little black quacking shapes
congregate on the cement path next to the creek.
Rolling my long white cane in front of me, I approach.
One by one, angered by my intrusion,
they vanish in a flurry of wings.

A Story After Noon

Flies buzz the table.
A cicada skitters back and forth.
Its incessant click click click draws near, fades away.
Cars rush by
while in the distance, hammers pound,
saws whine, dogs bark.
Hummingbirds flit about
with wings like weed eaters.
A mother admonishes her child to stay close
while the chatter of others permeates the air.
A lawn mower drones far away.
Birds chirp—a phone rings.
I hear other noises,
as I try and fail to write a nature poem.

On an Adventure with Her Grandkids

She drove into a mound
of freshly poured concrete surrounded by orange cones,
was cited by police for not following signage.
Her insurance company will be billed.
The blind aren't the only ones who blunder.

The Bark

What makes a dog bark?
It's something in the canine's anatomy.
Why do dogs bark?
They're excited, welcoming visitors,
warding off predators.

Why do dogs bark late at night?
They're left in the yard unattended.
Lonely, bored, cold,
once they're done relieving themselves,
they don't know what else to do
but make an incessant noise that grates on one's nerves for hours
until silenced by human intervention.

Is poetry like a barking dog?
In some ways, it is.
You read a poem, and you're stimulated—
but a bad poem can grate on your nerves
like a barking dog in the middle of the night.
Life is "ruff," isn't it?

I Dream of Murder at Sunrise

I enter the yard,
having been kept awake by the incessant barking.
I feel sorry for the pooch, left unattended.

It approaches me, tail wagging in welcome.
As I stroke the white, shaggy head,
I look toward the house for signs of life.

The dog sniffs my pocket.
I remove and unwrap a small portion of hamburger
with a generous amount of rat poison kneaded into the meat.
This will put the poor thing out of its misery, and mine, I think,
as I toss it on the ground.

The hound devours it,
lies down, closes its eyes,
is gone forever.

In a Pillow Case

You witness events around you.
Flung aside when not wanted,
you don't feel the rejection.
Happy to lie wherever you land,
you bask in the glow of the moment.

You don't feel the turmoil of lives changing.
You're just there, no matter what happens.
Through it all, you exist.

Florida's Song

When temperatures in Wyoming fall below zero,
and snow is on the ground, I go to Jupiter,
bask on a sunny beach,
feel the sand and water between my toes,

walk on the pier
while fishermen reel in large sharks and other sea creatures,
gaze at low flying birds,
view a poignant moment, as a man drops rose petals into the ocean
to honor his dead wife,

do water exercises in my brother's unheated outdoor pool
to the thumping rhythm of "Single Ladies."
enjoy a good book on the screened-in patio overlooking the pool
while a gentle breeze makes wind chimes sing a haunting melody.

On a warm Saturday, I go to Fort Lauderdale,
sail on The Jungle Queen to a tropical island,
eat a hot dog while others watch alligator wrestling.

After two weeks,
I return to the reality of winter in Wyoming.

Aprons

Flimsy white cloth garments
with either black or blue stripes on the bottom,
strings that tied at the neck,
these we put on in elementary school
because we were blind children who wore half of what we ate.

In eighth grade, we made them in a variety of colors
from one yard of tightly woven cotton fabric
with strings that tied at the waist.
Someone helped me make mine
because I was a blind girl who couldn't sew.

When I'm old, unable to care for myself,
I'll wear a shirt protector,
a soft terry cloth garment
with a Velcro fastener at the neck.

Part 4

In the End

Aging

I sit on a bench outside the nursing home,
an ordinary red brick building with many windows.
Oaks and cottonwoods grace the lawn.
The fragrance of roses and newly mown grass permeate the air.
Birds sing. Cars whoosh by.
Through an open window,
an old woman talks to herself, laughs.
I think of others imprisoned by age,
unable to stand, walk, talk, see, hear, think,
sentenced to a life of dependence for growing old.

A Losing Battle

My get up and go
just got up and went.
I'm feeling so down.
My whole life's been spent.

I sit in my chair
day in and day out.
Sometimes I cry.
Sometimes I shout.

I don't know one soul
from the next, don't you see?
I can only smile
when they talk to me.

I need help each day,
am unsure what to do.
Everything's jumbled.
Everything's new.

Although I can walk,
I don't know where to go.
Nothing's familiar.
There's nothing I know.

Sometimes it's hopeless.

I see no light
at the end of the tunnel,
no daybreak in sight.

It's just as well
there's no forthcoming dawn—
for my get up and go's
gotten up and gone.

Reta's Song

She sits in her wheelchair day in and day out,
singing the same song over and over and over again.
The tune is the same.
She makes up different words.
Sometimes, her words make sense.
Often, they have no meaning.
Unaware of what goes on around her,
she just keeps singing that same song
over and over and over again.

There was a time when she didn't sing,
not even when someone else was singing.
She'd talk your head off for hours.
She didn't keep singing that same song
over and over and over again.

She has changed.
She no longer talks your head off.
She sings it off.
When spoken to, she responds mostly In song.
The words are different.
The tune is the same.
She just keeps singing that same song
over and over and over again.

Fred

"How are you today?" I ask the old man in his wheelchair, as he smiles at me.

"Fit as a fiddle and ready for love," he answers.

He asks me the same questions. "What's your name? What's my name? Why am I here? Where's my wife? You're a beautiful girl. Do you have a husband?"

I could stay with him all day, repeat the answers to his questions—but I have places to go, things to do, people to see. With reluctance, I say goodbye.

Who's Coming Next?

Who will bathe, dress, feed me,
give me all my medications,
make sure I'm healthy?

Who will prepare and serve my meals,
pay attention to my requests for certain foods?

Who will play the guitar and sing,
encourage me to sing and exercise,
show me how to make Easter baskets,
call bingo, read to me?

Who will clean my room,
do my laundry, change my light bulbs?

Who will listen to my concerns,
help me work out my problems?

If you must leave,
who will take your place?

I Remember

In my childhood,
I helped Mother in the house,
went to school, was praised by teachers,
threatened with an eighteen-inch ruler,
played with siblings and friends,
was harassed by schoolyard bullies.

As a teen-ager, I went to high school,
to the prom, graduated.

In my adult years, I went to college,
got a job, was married.

When I grow old,
can't see, hear, or walk,
depend on others,
I'll remember my life.